THE FIGHTING
MAN OF JAPAN

A GROUP OF OFFICERS AND INSTRUCTORS AT THE IMPERIAL NAVAL COLLEGE, ETAJIMA, WITH THE AUTHOR AMONG THEM

THE FIGHTING MAN OF JAPAN

The Training and Exercises of the Samurai

F. J. NORMAN

DOVER PUBLICATIONS, INC.
Mineola, New York

Bibliographical Note

This Dover edition, first published in 2006, is an unabridged republication of the work originally published by Archibald Constable & Co., Ltd., London, in 1905.

International Standard Book Number: 0-486-44808-8

Manufactured in the United States of America
Dover Publications, Inc., 31 East 2nd Street, Mineola, N.Y. 11501

INTRODUCTION

THE author of the following brochure is an old soldier, who
has been for many years resident in Japan. While acting in
that country as an instructor in some of the leading colleges,
both military and civilian, he has had what are, perhaps,
unrivalled opportunities of making a thorough and systematic
study of the two "noble sciences" of *kenjutsu* and *jujutsu*.
The author is, so far as he is aware, the first Occidental who
has gone at all deeply into these two branches of Japanese
education. The benefit he has derived from their pursuit
has led him to the conviction that much advantage might
accrue to his native country from the introduction of exercises
so admirably calculated to improve the physique and also the
morale of its youth and manhood. The favourite games of
young England are necessarily restricted in practice to the
few, owing to the expensive nature of the requisite appliances,
the time-expenditure involved, and the cost of preparing the
ground. The majority can enjoy them only in the *rôle* of
spectators. Lookers on, it is said, see most of the game;
but neither *morale* nor physique are thereby greatly benefited,
and looking on is apt to degenerate into a dull pastime unless
relieved by betting. No such costly appliances are required
in connection with these Japanese exercises, in which all can
participate, without risk or danger to life, purse, or limb, but
with great benefit both to body and spirit. The following

INTRODUCTION

brief notes on the historical and practical side of *jujutsu* and *kenjutsu* make no pretence to being exhaustive, having been written rapidly with the express object of illustrating the general ideas and aims of the Japanese school of *jujutsu*. The author was unexpectedly summoned to assist the members of this school in giving a public demonstration of the art of *jujutsu* in Great Britain. The time placed at his disposal for writing and issuing the following brochure was limited, and he claims the indulgence of its readers both on that score and in consideration of the fact that the ground he has covered has hitherto been practically untrodden.

CONTENTS

ix

LIST OF ILLUSTRATIONS

LIST OF ILLUSTRATIONS

THE FIGHTING
MAN OF JAPAN

THE FIGHTING MAN
OF JAPAN

CHAPTER I

Commencement of Japanese Military History

THERE would appear to be little doubt that the two main causes contributing toward the fighting and sea-faring instincts of the Japanese are—first of all, the strong strain of Malay blood that runs in their veins ; and secondly, the favourable climatic conditions under which they have been bred and brought up. The Malay strain has given them evidently the necessary fire, bravery and dash for the calling of warriors ; to the second or climatic cause they owe those physical qualifications without which the advantage of race is often of so little avail. As regards the peculiar discipline and loyalty for which the Japanese have now become so famous, these traits would appear to be the outcome of their Mongolian blood and teachings ; for if there is one thing for which Far Orientals are distinguished more than another it is that marked deference and loyalty to the wishes of a superior, without which discipline can rest on no sure basis. It was

1

the introduction of Buddhism into the country, however, that gave the finishing touch to the character and ways of the Japanese warrior, as evolved in the shape of the *samurai*. Buddhistic teaching civilised and made a gentleman and a scholar of him, but never succeeded in spoiling him altogether for the rougher life of camps. For a century or so, it is true, the Japanese warrior appears to have been quite content with the newer ideas and teachings brought over from the mainland by the disciples of Shaka, yet, thoroughly and always manly at heart, he eventually got disgusted with their priestly rule; and so, taking the government of the country into his own hands again, he set to work applying his newly-gained knowledge to the feudalising of the national institutions.

With the introduction of feudalism into the country, the study of military arts and sciences spread apace among the " soldier gentry " of old Japan, and that is just what the *samurai* of old were. Japan has always turned to China for initiation and instruction upon the higher planes of thought and sentiment. And so it was to China that the *samurai* went in order to perfect themselves in their studies, but it was not long before they improved upon the teachings and methods of their models. And just why this should have been so may be gathered from the fact that while a Chinaman says: " One does not make a horse-shoe out of good iron, nor a soldier out of a good man," the Japanese say: *Hana wa sakura hito wa bushi;* or, " What the cherry is among flowers, so the *bushi* is among men." Or in other words —the cherry blossom being, in the estimation of the Japanese, the purest and noblest among flowers, so the *bushi*, or warrior, is the purest and noblest among men.

As a result of such high ideas, *bushido*, or "the way of the warrior," soon became, as it still is, a most important factor in the education, guidance and training of the Japanese soldier and official. But about this same *bushido* a great deal of nonsense has been written of late ; for, comparing it with the chivalry of the West, we find that while the European knight considered it his duty to respect women and the weakness and unpreparedness of a foe, the *bushi*, on the other hand, held to the maxim that " all is fair in love and war," and scrupled not to resort to devices of the most dishonourable kind in order to gain a desired object. And then, again, his sense of *giri*, or duty, never prevented a *bushi* from committing an evil act if such an act were only done in the service of his feudal lord. And much the same sort of thing held good even among the *samurai* women : as for instance when a mother sacrificed her younger children to save the life of her first-born, or a daughter consented to sell her chastity in order to pay the debts contracted by a dissipated father. All such, and many similar acts, were, and are still, allowable in Japan. It may be said, indeed, of our Japanese allies that they are firmly convinced that "the end justifies the means."

Until lately the *bushi* or *samurai* were easily distinguishable from the remainder of their fellow-countrymen, not less by their peculiar carriage of the body, begotten by the constant practice of martial exercises, than by the two swords stuck in those girdle sashes without which they never appeared in public. The longer of these two swords, the *katana*, was the *bushi's* main weapon of offence and defence, and the shorter, the *wakizashi*, or dirk, with a blade of from eight to twelve inches in length, was what they committed *hara-kiri* with.

3

[For an explanation of this see Chapter III.] Beside learning how to wield their swords aright all *bushi* underwent instruction in archery, the use of the halberd and lance, and in *jujutsu*; while many were, also, taught how to handle a boat, to swim, and to ride a horse. How to keep their weapons in order, how to bear pain, heat and cold, starvation and thirst, how to put up with the fewest possible wants—these are a few of the subjects of instruction included in the physical education of every true *bushi*. Along with his instruction in all these soldierly accomplishments every *bushi* received a scholastic and literary education, and in the case of many of them this was by no means of an inferior order. At first, as has already been noted, it was Buddhism and its teaching that attracted their allegiance; but later on, as Chinese became the classical language of the country, the Confucian Classics, the " Four Books " and the " Five Canons " took the place of the *Sutras*, and so continued to do until the advent of European ideas and civilisation. With the arrival of Mendez Pinto, the Portuguese navigator and discoverer of Japan, in 1542, the Japanese first learnt the use of firearms and fortifications. But while they appear to have readily adopted the Western system of fortifications, they were decidedly chary in taking to the musket; and why this was so may perhaps be explained by the fact that the harquebus of those days could have been little if at all superior to a well-strung bow, such as the Japanese seem to have had at that time. In range alone it may have been superior, but it is as likely as not that the Japanese bow possessed qualities superior in many other respects to that cumbersome and slow loading and firing shoulder piece. The precise character of the defensive works employed by the Japanese before 1542 is wrapped up in a good deal of mystery, though judging from the remarkable skill with which they now handle their wonderfully effective

PRINCE YAMATODAKE, ONE OF THE MOST FAMOUS
OF THE ANCIENT WARRIORS OF JAPAN

timbers, bamboos, and vines, and considering their Malay origin, it is most probable that stockades played a by no means unimportant part in them. I have been in many lands, but nowhere have I seen a country folk so clever in handling and rough-dressing timbers, and in making lashings out of creepers, as the Japanese, and certainly no creeper I have yet come across is so effective and generally useful for this last purpose as the wild wistaria of Japan. Freshly cut it is as pliable as a hempen cord, and when a lashing made of it has dried and hardened, then steel bands alone are superior to it.

It may, perhaps, be just as well to hark back here a little in order to show that the gift of military organisation is by no means a newly acquired art so far as the Japanese are concerned. For leaving out accounts dealing with the more apocryphal times, it is recorded of the aptly named Empress Jingo, that she organised and led an expedition against Korea in the year 200 A.D. But though the Emperor Sujin, 97–31 B.C., is said to have paid considerable attention to the subject of shipbuilding, yet there appears not to have been a sufficiency of sea-going craft in existence in Japan at that time for the warlike lady's purpose. Nothing daunted, she set to work building a perfect navy of transports ; just what they were like it is difficult to say, though there can be no doubt none of them were propelled by sail power.

Jingo Kogo's son Ojin, who is now worshipped in Japan as the " Spirit or God of War," is reported to have built a ship one hundred feet long. When completed it was tried at sea, and is said to " have been able to go through the water faster than a man could run on shore," and for this reason it was named *Karuno,* or the " Light One." When its timbers gave signs of giving out it was broken up, and with the exception of one piece, which was made into a *koto,* the so-called Japanese harp, the remainder was used as fuel for the production of sea-salt, the proceeds being applied to the building of new vessels. According to Japanese records there were at this time, upon one memorable occasion, no less than five hundred vessels collected in the harbour of Muko, but the tribute-bearer from Shiragi, one of the ancient divisions of Korea, that had been subdued by the dauntless Jingo, set them on fire—accidentally, it is said ; and in his anxiety to assist in repairing the mischief caused by his servant, the King of Shiragi sent over to Japan a number of clever naval architects. "From that time," say those same records, " the art of naval architecture became much improved and largely extended in Japan."

With the exception of a few short intervals of internal peace the Japanese appear to have passed their time, from the days of Jingo Kogo to the year 1275 A.D., in fighting among themselves, with the result that while families rose rapidly to power others sank no less rapidly. But in that year the Mongol Tartars, under Kublai Khan, having overthrown the reigning dynasty of China, and obtained the submission of all the surrounding states, commenced making haughty and unjust demands upon the Japanese. Rightly treating them with the contempt they deserved, the plucky islanders set to work preparing for the threatened invasion. The first attack made by the Mongols was upon Tsushima, but as this appears to have been repulsed without either side having incurred much loss, it may be taken for granted that it was nothing more than a feint in order to see of what stuff the defenders were made. Realising that he had to face a task of the most formidable character, Kublai Khan caused a number of warships to be built, of sizes and armaments unknown to the Japanese, and collecting an army of a

7

hundred thousand fighting men he approached, in the fourth month of the year 1281, the castle town of Daizafu. Nothing daunted, the Japanese attacked him, and, helped by a mighty typhoon, which drove a number of the Mongol ships ashore, they literally wiped out the great armada. Of the whole invading force, it is said, that only three men returned to China to tell the tale. So great was the renown won by the Japanese as the result of this, that, with the exception of a few European and American marines, Japan has never since then been offended by the sight of a successful invader.

For the next two and a half centuries, until the arrival of Mendez Pinto, the Japanese busied themselves with fighting among themselves, each feudal lord in his fastness being a law unto himself. But the arrival of Hideyoshi upon the scene, that Napoleon of Japan as he has been called, resulted in the centralising of the authority of the State in a single person. The many years' civil war had, however, let loose upon the country a host of armed men, inured to fighting, and too proud to work, with the result that something had to be done, and so the sapient and masterful Hideyoshi decided upon an invasion of Korea, as a preliminary to an invasion of China. What his undertaking was like may be realised from the fact that over half a million of men took part in his Korean adventure, and that this immense force kept the field for over two years, during which time it so harassed and devastated the country that when Hideyoshi died, in 1592, his generals were only too glad of an excuse to return to Japan. Following this event a series of civil wars again broke out in the country, and were only brought to a conclusion at the great battle of Sekigahara, when

Iyéyasu, in 1603, having defeated all his foes, seized the reins of power. For over two and a half centuries the Tokugawas, as Iyéyasu's family name was, ruled Japan with a sufficiently strong hand to prevent any undue disturbances

A MEDIEVAL WARRIOR

breaking out. Among one of the many means they devised to ensure this was the forcing the *daimyos*, or feudal lords, to repair to their capital once a year, and to leave hostages there while absent from it.

9

The arrival of Europeans in the country gave an immense impetus to the art of shipbuilding in Japan; but, true to their nature, the Japanese employed their newly gained knowledge more for other purposes than for peaceful pursuits, and their piratical raids upon Chinese shipping and along the China and Korean coasts developed to such an extent, that, to avoid a rupture with the governments of those two countries, the Shogun Iyemitsu, grandson of Iyéyasu, promulgated a law forbidding the building of ships above a certain tonnage. Had this law not been rigorously put into force, there is no saying what the Japanese empire might now have been. Siam, for instance, was for some years completely under the rule and guidance of certain Japanese adventurers, and a party of them even had the temerity to carry off into captivity the Dutch governor of Batavia. Some of them made their way to Madagascar and India, while others, joining hands with the Chinese pirates of Formosa, simply ruled that island and the waters about it. Just how these Vikings of the Far East were dreaded is amply exemplified by the numerous watch towers that still dot the whole of the North China coast, and also from the fact that despite the existence of many otherwise advantageous positions, all the coast towns and villages in Korea are—to use an Irishism—situated a few miles inland.

That the Spanish, Dutch, and other vessels which visited Japan from time to time were armed with cannon, may be taken for granted; but, curiously enough, the Japanese do not appear to have taken to these weapons or ordnance so readily as might have been supposed. Hideyoshi's troops certainly did use both large and small guns in their expedition against

10

the Koreans, but beyond mentioning the fact, none of the old records give satisfactory accounts of their so doing. We must not, however, lose sight of the fact that the Japanese have always been keen in-fighters, and that while all their old battles opened with discharges of arrows from both sides, this was invariably and quickly followed up by an advance of men skilled in the use of the spear, halberd and sword. Later on, toward the end of the seventeenth century, cannon were most effectually employed against the Christian rebels sheltering in the castle of Shimabara, but the guns in question were served (to their shame be it said) by Dutch gunners engaged by the Japanese authorities for this special purpose.

The arrival of the American squadron under Commodore Perry, in 1853, and its evolutions and gunnery practice, which that astute commander took very good care the Japanese should have every facility for seeing, opened the eyes of the Far Orient to the immense superiority of Occidental methods of warfare over their own; and the result was that factories were at once established at Yedo and elsewhere for the manufacture of arms and ammunition on the Western plan. Some of the wealthier feudal lords, not content with the slow progress made by these local houses in turning out arms and munitions of warfare, secretly purchased a quantity from the foreign merchants then commencing to do business in Japan. Perceiving the trend of Japanese thought, and recognising that much profit might accrue to their respective compatriots by cultivating it, the foreign representatives commenced a series of negotiations which ended in the Shogun's government applying for and obtaining the services of military and naval instructors from abroad. The first military mission was entirely French; but though it did excellent service, and undoubtedly laid the foundation for the present-day Japanese army, yet the revolution of 1868 and the disastrous result of the war of 1870 to the French colours induced the imperial authorities—who had by then taken the place of the Shogunate in the government of the empire—to engage German instructors in their place as the contracts of its various members lapsed. That these last did their duty there can be no doubt, but they achieved nothing like the success that has been so generally claimed for them, for there can be no disputing the fact that the Japanese army gained greater advantages from the swarm of officers sent to study in Europe than from any instructions it may ever have received from its imported instructors. And to say that the Japanese army tactics or organisation are copies of the German is to advance a claim that is absurd; for if they have not adopted more from the French, they certainly have adapted so much from other and various continental armies that the German share in it is but a fraction of the whole. Fighters and military organisers the Japanese have always been, as I have endeavoured to show; and so all they had to learn, though that certainly was all-important, and yet not so difficult considering their military instincts, was how to employ to the best advantage the new arms and tactics then adopted by them. How quickly and how intelligently they picked up the knack of so doing may be gathered from the fact that when the rebellious Nagato forces invaded Buzen and Bungo, in 1866, the commander and officers of the gunboat *Slaney*, who witnessed the embarkation and disembarkation of the force, declared afterward that "it was all executed in a manner that would have done credit to the best European troops."

Contrary to generally-accepted ideas upon the subject, to the Dutch, and not to the English, must be credited the first foreign attempt at training a Japanese naval force; though, at the same time, to the Portuguese and Spanish friars of the sixteenth century must be credited the first instructions given to the Far Easterners in the art of ship-building, as understood in the West, and in the science of navigation. What may justly be considered as of peculiar interest to all Englishmen is the fact that Will Adams, a fellow-countryman of theirs, who landed in Japan in April, 1600, was retained at the Court of Iyéyasu, the then Shogun, as a ship-builder, instructor of navigation, and as a sort of diplomatic agent when other English and Dutch traders began to arrive in the country. Considering how very much the Japanese are indebted to British instructions, help, and advice with regard to their naval matters, it is a curious coincidence, surely, that Will Adams's grave, at Hemi, is situated on the heights overlooking the present great naval yard of Yokosuka.

Not until two years after the abolition of feudalism, in 1869, did the Japanese think of organising a national navy, though just before this both the Shogun's government and the leading Daimyōs possessed navies of their own. But these were composed of all sorts and conditions of vessels, from those of purely native style to others of European build and armament, though when of the latter they were seldom other than converted merchant ships and steamers. One or two possessed by the Shogun were, however, specially-built

war vessels, and the first that was so built for him was the
"Kaiyo-maru," a composite gun-boat of about one thousand
tons burden, built in Holland. In 1858 the steam-yacht
"Emperor" was presented to the Shogun by Lord Elgin, on
behalf of the British Government, "as a token of its friend-
ship and goodwill" upon the signing of the first treaty
between England and Japan. Ten years later the United

A VESSEL BUILT BY WILL ADAMS FOR THE JAPANESE
ABOUT 1600 A.D.

States Government handed over to the newly-constituted
Imperial Government the iron-clad frigate "Stonewall Jack-
son" as a sort of sop for the scandalous treatment meted out
to the then late Shogun, who had prepaid certain American
contractors for a ship-of-war; when this vessel arrived in
Japan the Japanese authorities, seeing it was not worth a
quarter of the sum advanced, refused to take it over, and

14

getting no redress from the United States representative in Japan, sent a mission to New York about the matter, with the aforegoing result. That there was some very unpleasant scandal behind the whole affair there can be no doubt, for it is difficult to understand how the United States Government was reimbursed the difference between the value of the two ships.

A FIGHT TO THE DEATH

CHAPTER II

The Education of Japanese Military and Naval Officers.

LEAVING out of consideration the little knowledge the Japanese picked up of navigation from their early Portuguese, Dutch, and English visitors during the sixteenth and seventeenth centuries, it was not until the early part of the late eighteen-sixties that a small naval mission was despatched by the Shogun's government to Holland, and it was the members of this mission, assisted by some Dutch officers and men, who brought the "Kaiyo-maru," already mentioned, to Japan. In 1867 the same Shogun's government applied for and obtained the services of a number of British officers and men as naval instructors. Unfortunately, however, this mission, under the leadership of Commander Tracey, R.N., had to be withdrawn by the British authorities because of the revolution which broke out a few months after its arrival in Japan, leading to the effectual overthrow of the Shogun's power. During the troublous times antecedent to and following the revolution, when no one knew exactly what was to follow, certain of the great Daimyōs set to work organising their forces, naval as well as military. " One of them," as Professor Chamberlain says, " the Prince of Hizen, eager to possess a navy of his own, engaged Lieutenant Hawes, of the

Royal Marines, as gunnery instructor on board a vessel named the 'Ryūjō Kan'; and this officer, who had an unusual talent for organisation, and who occupied himself, both on board the 'Ryūjō Kan' and later on in other positions, with many matters besides gunnery and the training of marines, may be considered the real father of the Japanese navy."

When matters had somewhat quieted down, the new government, the Mikado's in contradistinction to the late Shogun's, applied to the British authorities for the services of a second naval mission, and as a result of this a party of officers and men under Commander Douglas, R.N., set out for and arrived in Japan in 1873. A naval college was formed at Tokyo, and after a certain number of picked officers and men had received the necessary instructions in gunnery, seamanship, &c., they were taken for a cruise to Australia and the islands between it and Japan. The work done was decidedly good, but needless to say some little friction arose at times between the instructors and the instructed, and more especially so with regard to matters of discipline. For it must here be explained that Japanese ideas of discipline at that time, though good enough in their way, were very different to what they now are. After putting in six years' service in Japan, this second naval mission returned to England, leaving behind, however, one or two officers and petty-officers as employees of the Japanese government.

In the early eighties the Naval College was removed to Etajima, in the Inland Sea, and an Academy, or Staff College, for officers, was established at Tokyo at the same time, while gunnery and torpedo schools were also organised. Candidature to the Naval College at Etajima is open to every male subject of the Mikado, with certain limitations as regards age, character and physique. Aspirants must be between fifteen and twenty years of age, and after furnishing the authorities with the requisite "character certificates" they are called upon to undergo a physical examination at the hands of a committee of naval surgeons, after which the entrance examinations take place. As the majority of such aspirants have been thoroughly coached at schools which make a speciality of such work the competition between them at the annual entrance examinations is invariably particularly keen. From 20 to 25 per cent. fail to satisfy the demands of the doctors, and of the remainder only about 10 per cent. succeed in passing the entrance examination. Having taken a part in many such examinations I can safely state that they are absolutely fairly conducted. The compulsory subjects are :—Under the head of mathematics—arithmetic, algebra, plane geometry, and plane trigonometry ; under the head of Japanese—literature and composition ; under the head of English—grammar, conversation, translation of Japanese into English and English into Japanese ; under the head of physics—chemistry, natural history and physical geography ; under the head of drawing and sketching —draughtsmanship both freehand and mechanical. There are besides a number of optional subjects, such as the Chinese, French, German, and Russian languages, marks awarded for which help the candidate—not so much to pass into the College as to secure a good position on the list of successful candidates. Once entered the College no cadet is

18

allowed to resign under any pretext whatsoever; but should
the authorities find one of the cadets wanting either physically
or in character and ability, that cadet is at once dismissed, and

AN ETAJIMA CADET

in my three years' experience of Etajima I only remember
two of them being so dismissed the College. Both these
two were discharged for physical reasons; one because of
failing eyesight, and the other because the surgeon in charge

19

thought he detected signs of consumption in him. But, as a matter of fact, the surgeon was wrong, for young Beppu, a particularly nice lad, then went in for the army, and is now an artilleryman of great promise.

A better situation for a Naval College than Etajima it would indeed be difficult to find, for, in the first place, it is, as the termination to its name implies, an island, and though within easy reach of Kure and Hiroshima, yet so placed as to be well off the beaten track. So irregularly shaped is this island that Etajima Bay is well-nigh land-locked, and the College stands in ample grounds, with hills to the north, south, and east of it, and the waters of the bay to the west. The staff of officers and instructors is particularly large, the President being an admiral. In my days the course was a four-year one, but it has now been reduced to three years. During the first year four hours a week are given to gunnery, four to seamanship, one to engineering, six to English, five to physics, six to mathematics, making a total of twenty-six hours' study a week. Besides all this the cadet has at least an hour's drill a day, and receives instructions in *jujutsu*, fencing, gymnastics, rowing, &c. He will be required to get up within half-an-hour of sunrise, and will be served with breakfast at 7.30, lunch at noon, and dinner at 5.30 p.m. All work and studies are carried out in clean and neat white slop suits. Only on Sundays are the cadets allowed out of the College grounds, and even then for never more than three hours in the morning and three hours in the afternoon. Each class has its own club outside the College grounds, usually a farm house, where members of it may and do indulge in a little extra feeding, drinking and smoking, and, what is not allowed them whilst in the College grounds, in the reading of newspapers. The discipline kept is decidedly good, though to an average English youth it would be irksome beyond measure. Considering the advantages existing at Etajima it certainly is curious (and perhaps instructive) that none of the cadets ever think of going in for a little shooting or fishing ; but then the Japanese are not a sportingly-inclined people. On one or two occasions I took a cadet or two out shooting or fishing with me, but it was easy to see that his heart was never in the sport; and this was the more remarkable, for such children of the officers, boys or girls, as I took out from time to time simply revelled in the delights of a day's shooting or fishing.

During the cadets' second year four hours a week are given to gunnery, three to seamanship, one to torpedo instruction, three to navigation, three to engineering, six to English, three to physics, and five to mathematics. During the third, or final, year, three hours a week are given to gunnery, four to seamanship, four to torpedo instruction, seven to navigation, one to engineering, six to English, and three to mechanics. Under the heading of seamanship are included instructions in the international rule of the road at sea, signalling, shipbuilding, provisioning and other kindred matters, and under the head of navigation the cadet has to study meteorology, surveying and the like. Beside all this the cadet will from time to time attend lectures upon international and civil law; his naval history he gets up mostly while studying English. The training ship, launches, boats, the battery and the model rooms at Etajima are all thoroughly "up-to-date," and the instructions

21

conveyed through their medium are practical and to the point.

Passing out of the College the cadet is promoted to mid-shipman, and is then, with a number of his class-mates, posted to one of the cruisers specially fitted up for the purpose. In my days the two cruisers that were so fitted up were the "Hiyei" and the "Kongo," but as the classes have now grown from sixty to two hundred three vessels are detailed for this purpose: the "Matsushima," the "Itsuku-shima" and the "Hashidate," sister ships of 4,200 tons. When all is ready these vessels start on a cruise lasting from six to eight months, and on returning to Japan the midshipmen are distributed among ships in commission. Two very good points to be here noted are that while a certain number of civilian instructors are attached to the College the greater part of the instructional work is carried out by naval officers, and that when a class has finished its three years' course a number of officers who have worked with them at the College accompany them on their finishing cruise.

At the end of a year or two the midshipman is promoted to a sub-lieutenancy, but only after having passed certain prescribed examinations. A Japanese naval sub-lieutenant is perhaps as hard worked an individual as exists, for not only has he to take his full share of watches and drills, but he is constantly being called upon to write reports and essays upon all sorts of matters, professional and otherwise; but despite this last fact it is truly remarkable how little the Japanese naval officer is capable of discussing subjects other than purely professional ones.

In two to four years' time the sub-lieutenant gets his lieutenancy, and if after a while he is reported upon favourably he is sent to the Naval Academy at Tokyo for a course in higher naval duties. Specially selected lieutenants go through a two years' course called "Koshu," and as this is done with a view to their after employment upon the staff, the subjects studied are strategy and tactics—naval and military; naval history; fortifications; law; international law and diplomatic usages and history; military and naval administration; political economy; gunnery; torpedo; navigation; ship building, and engineering. While undergoing this remarkably thorough and comprehensive course the officers are sent from time to time to take part in various manœuvres, to visit ships, forts, naval stations and factories when the same are being inspected by experts. Other lieutenants go through a course named "Otsushu," lasting one year, during the course of which they go in for the higher study of gunnery, torpedo and navigation duties. The idea governing this course is to turn out specialists in some one of the subjects named. Captains, commanders and senior lieutenants who have become a little rusty in certain subjects are allowed to attend a course called "Senka," but only so if it is considered they will truly benefit by so doing. Should an officer show special adaptability for a certain subject, and yet be lacking in others that might otherwise fit him for a staff appointment, he is put through a course called "Koshiuka." Besides these courses officers and men are constantly being put through practical courses at the schools of gunnery and torpedo at Yokosuka, and in addition to all this, special courses are formed for instruction in new weapons and scientific instruments for use with the same.

The non-executive branches of the Navy are particularly well provided for as regards instruction by special schools of their own. The Engineers' College at Yokosuka, and the rules regulating entrance to it, and the course of studies there, are based on lines similar to those that hold good with respect to the Naval College at Etajima. Yokosuka being a great dockyard and arsenal the College is therefore well situated for its purpose. Candidates for the Paymaster's Department are mainly recruited from graduates of the Imperial University, and after passing a course at the Paymaster's Training School at Tokyo they are first posted to ships in commission and later on to such as the exigencies of the service may demand. Petty officers and men, who are otherwise smart and useful but lacking in education, are also sent for a while to the Paymaster's Training School for educational purposes, as also are writers, cooks, etc.

While the officers of the Japanese Navy are recruited mainly from the best families in the empire, the men are recruited from its fisher folk, sea-faring and farming classes, and the result is that its personnel is of a very high order indeed. And though there is a good deal of heart-burning at times among a large section of the commissioned class, due to the all-predominating influence of the Satsuma element, yet on the other hand one never hears of those disgraceful bullyings and scenes among the seamen that are only too rife among the Mikado's soldiery. This is probably due to the fact that while the bluejackets are all recruited from much the same type of men, his soldiers are taken from all sections of

Japanese life, and so less cause for friction exists among the sailors than among the soldiers. That the Navy is the favourite branch of the service in Japan there can be no doubt, and the result is that a very goodly proportion of the men in it are volunteers and not (as in the Army) conscripts. A fearful lot of gush and nonsense has been written recently of the joy with which the Japanese conscripts join headquarters; but all who have lived among the people of the land know only too well that this joy is too often very much put on, and that while the majority of the bluejackets go back to civil life with some useful calling learnt while serving their time, the average soldier returns to it a spoilt and dissatisfied man.

The education of the Japanese military officer is as thorough as is the education of his comrade in the navy, and like him, too, he is mainly recruited from the better class *samurai* families. Unlike the naval officer, however, he has more than one way open to him for gaining a commission, at least during the first stages of his career. He may commence by graduating out of one of the many recognised Cadet Schools of the empire; or by graduating out of any Middle School, licensed and recognised by the government; or if he can produce an educational certificate of the same value as that of a graduate's from a Middle School. In both these last two cases, however, an aspirant for a commission must obtain a nomination from the officer commanding the regiment or corps he is desirous of joining. Should he succeed in doing so, and is otherwise qualified, he then joins his regiment or corps as an "officer candidate," and as such is required to put in at least twelve months' service in the ranks in order to gain a complete and practical experience of all the duties of a soldier. Having done so to the entire satisfaction of his commanding officer he will next be drafted to the Military College, Tokyo, for an eighteen months' course in military arts and sciences, and should he at the end of it be approved by a committee of officers he will be granted his commission as a sub-lieutenant. While serving his twelve months in the ranks the " candidate " has to perform his share of guards, drills, &c., but instead of living and messing in a common barrack room he will share one with other " candidates," and though drawing no pay during the whole of that time he will be supplied with all the necessary kit, rations, &c., at the government's expense.

The Military College is divided into a number of sections, in each of which special attention is devoted to a certain branch of the service, such as infantry, cavalry, field and fortress artillery, engineering and train, the " officer candidate " joining that section representative of his own particular branch. The " candidate students," as they are then called, are divided into three companies, each under the command of a captain, and each company is divided into six sections with lieutenants in charge. The sections are from twenty-five to thirty strong, and each " candidate student " in it is in his turn head or chief of it, and the extraordinary seriousness and earnestness with which they then perform their duties must be seen to be duly appreciated. While the drill and exercises, &c., taught are in keeping with that branch of the service the " candidate student " aspires to be a member of, all the candidates alike study tactics, topo-graphy, military administration, field hygiene, &c., but no foreign language in particular, as is the case with their comrades of the navy. At the close of every year a grand

A CAVALRY LIEUTENANT OF THE IMPERIAL BODYGUARD

graduating ceremony is held, which the Emperor and all his high officers of state make a point of attending.

After two years' service as sub-lieutenant the Japanese officer receives his promotion to a lieutenancy, and should he have shown special keenness and aptitude for his calling he is then sent for a course of study to the Military Staff College. The course there is a three years' one, and a remarkably comprehensive one, too, the officers going through it being attached from time to time to branches of the service other than their own. Those that pass with success receive diplomas and distinctive badges that they wear ever afterwards ; these badges distinguish them most markedly from their brother officers who have not gone through a similar ordeal. From officers trained thus the staff of the Japanese army is recruited ; with what happy results has been most signally shown during the late war.

Besides the Staff College each branch of the service in the Japanese army has its own particular school of instruction, and then there is for all of them the Toyama Military College, where officers, non-commissioned officers and men are put through courses of tactics, gymnastics, fencing, musketry, gunnery, &c. But while so much is done for the education and training of the combatant ranks the non-combatants are not forgotten. Military surgeons for instance complete their training at the Army Medical College, and this after graduating from the Medical College, Imperial University. The veterinary surgeons are recruited from graduates of the Agricultural College, Komeba, receiving an after and finishing education at the Army Veterinary School, Tokyo. Military intendants and paymasters are trained at the Military Administration College.

With regard to the training of the rank and file of the

Japanese army and navy, it may here be pointed out, little or no attention is paid by the officers to the teaching of parade and show movements to their men, or to what is so generally and so falsely termed " smartness " among us, and perhaps more especially so is this the case when we come to such matters as relate to the instructions given the recruit in the use of the sword and bayonet. Loose play and plenty of it is invariably their rule, and so, though a squad of Japanese soldiers or sailors may not be able to go through the sword or bayonet exercise with the same precision as a squad of our guardsmen, it will certainly be found that far and away a greater proportion of them will know how to use the weapons they are armed with better and more effectively. Women not occupying the position in Japanese society they do in the West, little or no pains are taken by the military authorities of the Mikado to cater for their amusement, and the result is one never sees any " Agricultural Hall tomfoolery " in Japan.

Having decided, in 1868, upon Westernising the governmental institutions of the empire, the Japanese Government there and then adopted the continental system of universal conscription. What a bold step to take this was may be realised by appreciating the fact that, not only did the *samurai* of those days regard the following of arms as their own peculiar prerogative, but the country, as a result of the abolition of feudalism, was over-run by hordes of these men, whose chances of martial occupation seemed gone for ever. Unfortunately for themselves, however, not only were the lower class *samurai* averse to the bearing and use of Western arms, but they were also so imbued with the clan spirit and jealousies of the

29

time that the gathering together of a number of them in barracks would inevitably have resulted in fights and quarrels innumerable. And so it came about that while the officers and non-commissioned officers of the newly organised national army were recruited solely from the ranks of the better-class *samurai*, the men were mostly recruited from the sturdy farmer and artisan classes of the land; but as the necessity for a larger army arose, as a result of the French, German and Russian interference over the Liaotung Peninsula affair of 1895, merchants and even the much despised actor and other classes were drawn upon to supply the necessary number of recruits for the Mikado's army.

Sent on service for the first time in 1876-77, to suppress the Satsuma rebellion, the newly organised national army did not do quite so well as might have been supposed, but then, it must be remembered, it was called upon to face veteran soldiers of the same race as the men composing it, and, moreover, " veteran soldiers " belonging to the most warlike of all the clans of old Japan, and with all the prestige of a successful revolution behind them, and with much of the sympathy of the nation to encourage them. The result was that as the newly-raised troops had not then learnt either to shoot straight or to use their bayonets aright, the Satsuma swordsmen often proved themselves more than a match for them. Perceiving this, and being fully alive to the necessity for taking prompt measures, the government commenced enlisting a number of the old-time style of Japanese swords-men, and these with the police, who were all *samurai*, and therefore good swordsmen too, soon put an end to the revolution and the lives of thousands of their plucky but misguided fellow-countrymen. A few years later, however, the new army did remarkably well in the Formosan affair, and what a good account it gave of itself in China in 1894-95, and again in 1900, is now a matter for history; its recent marvellous doings against the Russians have gained for it the world-renowned fame it so well deserves.

CHAPTER III

" Kenjutsu," or Japanese Fencing

IN few countries has the sword had so much attention and honour paid it as in Japan; for regarded as being of divine origin, it has been worshipped as such. In the interests of veracity it must further be admitted that few swordsmen in other lands have, from a European standpoint, so defiled their blades as those of Japan. For instance, it was quite a common occurrence, even so lately as the seventies of the last century, for a *samurai*, or gentleman soldier of old Japan, to pay a small fee to the public executioner for the privilege of being allowed to test his blade upon the carcase of a criminal, and even at times upon the living body of one. And some Japanese swordsmen, with the same object in view, went further than this, and hesitated not to resort to what they so expressively termed " cross-roadcutting," the victim in such a case being generally a beggar—man, woman, or child, it mattered not which to them.

The very old-time Japanese sword, the *tsurugi*, was a very different sort of weapon to what one now sees in museums and on sale at curio shops in England. It had a straight, double-edged blade, some three feet or more in length, and was not so unlike the sword of the Western knight of old. The *katana*, the mediæval and modern sword of Japan, is a much lighter and shorter weapon, with a single-edged blade slightly curving toward the point. Worn with the *katana*, but by *samurai* alone, was the *wakizashi*, a dirk with a blade of from eight to twelve inches in length, and it was with this that the *hara-kiri*, or "happy dispatch," as it has been termed, was performed.

Curiously enough the word *hara-kiri*, though made up from two Japanese words, *hara* or belly and *kiri* or cutting, is of European invention. No Japanese, except in joke and at the expense of the foreigner, ever thinks of using the term, always preferring the synonym *seppuku*. There were two kinds of *seppuku*, — obligatory and voluntary, and as Professor Chamberlain says, in his " Things Japanese," with respect to this subject :—" The former was a boon granted by the government, who graciously permitted criminals of the Samurai class to destroy themselves instead of being handed over to the common executioner. Time and place were officially notified to the condemned, and officials were sent to witness the ceremony. This custom is quite extinct. Voluntary *hara-kiri* was practised by men in hopeless trouble, also out of loyalty to a dead superior." And then the Professor goes on to give some well-known examples of this last :— " Examples of this class still take place ; one was mentioned in the newspapers of April of this very year, 1901, and two others in May. That of a young man called Ohara Takeyoshi, which occurred in 1891, is typical. He was a lieutenant in the Yezo militia, and ripped himself up in front of the graves of his ancestors at the temple of Saitokuji, in Tokyo. Following the usual routine in such cases, Lieutenant Ōhara left a paper setting forth the motives of his act, the only innovation being that this document was directed to be forwarded to the Tokyo News Agency for publication in all the newspapers. The writer, it seems, had brooded for eleven years over the likelihood of Russian encroachment in the northern portion of the Japanese empire, and feeling that his living words and efforts were doomed to fruitlessness, resolved to try what his death might effect. In this particular instance no result was obtained. Nevertheless, Ōhara's self-sacrifice, its origin in political considerations, and the expectation that an appeal from the grave would move men's hearts more surely than any arguments urged by a living voice—all this was in complete accord with Japanese ways of thinking. The government had no sooner yielded to the demands of France, Russia, and Germany, by giving up the conquered province of Liaotung, than forty military men committed suicide in the ancient way. Even women are found ready to kill themselves for loyalty and duty, but the approved method in their case is cutting the throat. Nowise strange, but admirable to Japanese ideas, was it that when, in 1895, the news of Lieutenant Asada's death on the battle-field, was brought to his young wife, she at once, and with her father's consent, resolved to follow him. Having thoroughly cleansed the house and arrayed herself in her costliest robes, she placed her husband's portrait in the alcove, and prostrating herself before it, cut her throat with a dagger that had been a wedding gift."

Just what gave rise to the custom of *seppuku* it is difficult to say, but it probably had its origin in the desire of vanquished warriors to avoid the humiliations of falling into their enemies' hands alive. This was, undoubtedly, the case in the many instances one heard of at the commencement of

34

the late war in the Far East, when Japanese officers and men committed *seppuku* by hundreds to escape being made prisoners of war by the Russians. The young *samurai* of old, besides learning how to use his weapons aright, was also taught how to perform *seppuku* in the approved fashion, which was as follows: Having bathed and taken leave of

A SAMURAI ABOUT TO PERFORM SEPPUKU

his friends, the would-be suicide then spread a rug or sheet or something of the sort on the matted floor of his room, and sitting down in front of the alcove, facing his family tablets, he then unclothed the upper portion of his body—down to the waist. Tucking the disengaged garments under and behind his thighs, he then took his *wakizashi*, and unsheathing it, pressed the blade to his forehead while he bowed forward, and toward the tablets. Then grasping the dirk by

35

the right hand he plunged the blade deeply into his belly, and with the assistance of the left hand, helped to draw it across it. The disengaged garments tucked under his thighs prevented his falling backwards when he could no longer sit upright through pain and weakness, that being considered anything but a proper way for a *samurai* to fall. The women's *seppuku* was carried out more by a stab in the throat than a direct cutting of it, and in their case their garments were so fastened around by a cord as to minimise all chances of the same becoming dissarranged during their final death struggles.

" Cherished by the *samurai* as almost part of his own self, and considered by the common people as their protector against violence, what wonder," says Mr. McClatchie, "that we should find it [the sword] spoken of in glowing terms by Japanese writers as 'the precious possession of lord and vassal from time older than the divine period,' or as ' the living soul of the *samurai* ' ? " And again, what wonder that the Japanese should have many a good sword story to tell. One told me by my old fencing master is not only interesting and amusing, but also thoroughly illustrative of the grim humour of the *samurai* with regard to the testing of sword blades, and is as follows : According to him, there lived in days gone by a certain *daimyo*, or feudal lord, who was a great patron of swordsmiths and swordsmen. One day a swordsmith in his service presented him with a beautiful blade he had but just lately finished. Desirous of seeing it tested the *daimyo* sent for the crack swordsman among his retainers, and upon his arrival ordered him to test the blade upon the body of a fish hawker who chanced to be passing along a road lying within

the precincts of the castle.　Putting the sword in his girdle
in the place of his own, which he left behind him in the

A SAMURAI IN CEREMONIAL COSTUME

charge of a friend, the great swordsman strutted off down the
road, met and passed the fish-hawker, and then returned to

his feudal lord by another and shorter road. Furious with him the *daimyo* asked why he had not carried out the instructions given him? Begging his lord to have patience, the swordsman asked him to watch the fish-hawker carefully when he came to a certain sharp turning in the road. This he did, and to his wondering surprise saw him collapse all of a sudden, for while the upper portion of his body toppled over one way the lower half fell another. The moral attached to the story is, of course, that not only was the sword an unusually fine one, but the swordsman who wielded it so dexterous, and with so true an edge had he made his cut, that it only required the twisting swing of the fish-baskets to finish his job.

Up to 1876 all *samurai* wore two swords, that being their particular mark of distinction, and the different ways of carrying the weapon indicated the rank of the wearer. Men of high birth wore theirs with the hilt pointing straight upwards; the common people, who were only allowed to wear one sword, and then too, only when on a journey, wore theirs stuck horizontally in the *obi*, or girdle-like sash of the Japanese; while ordinary *samurai* wore theirs in a position about half-way between the other two. To clash the sheath of one's sword against that belonging to another person was held to be a grave breach of etiquette; to turn the sheath in the belt, as though about to draw, was tantamount to a challenge; while to lay one's weapon on the floor of a room, and to kick the guard with the foot in the direction of anyone else, was a deadly insult that generally resulted in a combat to the death. It was not even thought polite to draw a sword from its sheath without begging the permission of

38

any other person present. A Japanese gentleman of the old school calling on another, even though he might be his most intimate friend, invariably left his sword with the door-keeper of the house, so little did such men, apparently, trust each other.

As I believe that I was the first Occidental to make a

ILL-TIMED POINT AND RESULT

study of Japanese swordsmanship, it may be of interest if I here describe my experiences in the fencing schools of Tokyo; and so to begin: the summer of 1888 found me established in Tokyo, and as the sedentary nature of my duties commenced to tell on my health, I decided to take up the study of *Kenjutsu*, or Japanese fencing. Getting into touch with the authorities at the Keishicho, or head police

station of Tokyo, I soon secured an introduction to Umezawa-san, the fencing master of the Takanawa Police Station,
and then quite one of the best swordsmen in Japan. Never

THE AUTHOR AND UMEZAWA-SAN.

did a *maitre d'armes* take more interest and pride in a
pupil than Umezawa did in me, and this was all the more
commendable on his part, because the majority of the
fencing masters in Tokyo looked upon his teaching me
Japanese swordsmanship as a sort of renegade act. The

first dozen lessons or so were given me on the little lawn
in front of my house, but after a while I used to attend
daily at the Takanawa fencing-room, and for a couple of

A SIDE-SLIP, AND WHAT WOULD HAPPEN

months or so fenced with, or rather took instructions from,
the best fencers attending there. When he thought I was
sufficiently advanced Umezawa set me to fence with some of
the more indifferent and harder hitting swordsmen, but was
always close at hand to give instructions and to correct

41

faults. Writing as an old cavalry man, with plenty of experience of regimental drill grounds and gymnasiums, I can safely say that the Japanese system of teaching swordsmanship is far and away superior to the absurd sword-exercise system in vogue in the British army, and that for rough dismounted work the Japanese system of two-handed swordsmanship is much superior to any of the systems of Europe. A first-class French or Italian duellist would, more than probably, beat a first-class Japanese swordsman, but only so if fighting on ground thoroughly suitable to his own peculiar style of sword-play. On rough ground, on a hill side, or on ground covered with impedimenta, the Japanese swordsman would more than likely have the advantage ; or in other words, in positions where a rough-and-tumble fight is going on, and where men want to kill, and kill quickly, without attending too much to details of form over it.

As a weapon of offence and defence a *katana* is an infinitely superior one to the ridiculous, single-handed sword with its 36-inch blade, with which British infantry officers are armed, and with slight modifications in its make and use the *katana* could be rendered still more effective. In the first place, its blade is considerably shorter—from ten to fifteen inches—thus allowing for the majority of men greater freedom of movement; for nobody can deny that to a dismounted man a long scabbard is a horrible nuisance, and that to a shortishly-inclined man it is an absolute incumbrance. But though shorter in the blade the *katana* has a longer grip, and when one has learnt to use it aright it is truly wonderful what little length of reach is lost. This great length of grip permits of the use of both hands for the purpose of delivering a crushing blow or cut; and, moreover, after practising the Japanese style of fencing, a swordsman becomes quite ambidextrous. How very disconcerting this last is to an opponent all swordsmen are fully aware, and when to this is added the fact that *katana* play is a closer play than that of the cut-and-thrust sword of the Occident, it must be admitted that it is an infinitely superior one to it for the one and great purpose of a fight to the death. It certainly is not so taking to the eye as—let us

I. ONODA

say—a French or Italian swordsman's play; but while there is less ostentatious art and ceremony about it, there certainly is just as much science, and it may also be added as much, if not more, deadly intent.

Among the many swordsmen who used to put in their daily attendance at the Takanawa fencing-room was one who very early attracted my attention. He was an elderly man, and in some respects a finer swordsman than Umezawa, who introduced him to me one day as his *sensei* or teacher. Onoda was his name, and though he was exceedingly tall for a

43

Japanese he was quite the best built one I have come across. For a long time I could gather nothing more about him than that he did not like foreigners, and that it would be just as well if I did not thrust my acquaintanceship upon him. Later on I learnt that he was, or had been, the hereditary fencing master to the late Shogun or "generalissimo" of Japan. All this, of course, helped to arouse my curiosity, but a grimmer or more forbidding-looking old man never lived than Onoda-sensei; and so what was my surprise when, some six months after I had begun learning *kenjutsu*, he came up to me one afternoon and, presenting his card, as shown on page 43, offered to take me on for a bout. Delighted at the thought, I was soon ready, but no sooner did the other fencers in the room see what was going to happen than they stopped fencing ; and, making quite a ring round us, stood looking on with what I could not help thinking were quite troubled faces. They knew well that Onoda-san had highly disapproved of my being admitted to the fencing-room, and I am not sure but that some of them did not think my days were about to be numbered. They were quite wrong, and Onoda-san and myself got on so well after this that, instead of keeping aloof from me any longer, he rather sought me out than otherwise for my company. In his way, he was a most peculiar old fellow, a sort of Buddhist puritan, and when he found out I had spent some years in India he was for ever asking me questions about it, its people and their religions, &c. He did a thing one day I never knew another adult Japanese to do, (though I have known one or two of my very young friends among them do a similar thing), and that was to reprove a fellow-countryman of his for being rude to me and calling out

44

after me in the streets. Being an old *samurai*, with an exceptionally fine presence and manner, he did this in a way that sent that erring individual literally grovelling in the dust of the road. With such a man as my friend and instructor, I

MEMBERS OF THE TAKANAWA FENCING SCHOOL

soon was more than able to hold my own with the average good swordsmen of Tokyo, and remarkably useful I found the power of being able to do so, for it brought me into contact with a class of Japanese that few, if any other foreigners have ever had the chance of becoming acquainted with. However, to revert to the *kenjutsu*.

The *kabuto*, or helmet, is in many respects superior to the mask worn by the sabre-players of Europe, but while it gives ample protection to the face, neck, and throat, it does not sufficiently protect the sides of the head, nor yet its top or crown. It sits much firmer, however, than do any of our fencing helmets or masks, being tied, or rather lashed, on to the head. Under it is invariably worn a *tenugui*, or small native towel, wrapped round the head in turban-like fashion, as shown in the photograph, in which I am seen standing by the side of Umezawa-san. The reason for this is of a purely cleanly or sanitary nature, and the result is that no Japanese helmets ever have an unpleasant odour.

The *do*, or corselet, is a lighter, cooler, and in every way a far superior chest and body protector to the leather jerkins of European sabre-players. It is made of slips of the very best and soundest of bamboos, strung perpendicularly together in the required shape, and trimmed and strengthened with fastenings of leather, silk, or hemp. The best *do* are lacquered with the *mon* or crest of the owner, and remarkably handsome some of them are. They are worn hanging somewhat loosely, being suspended from the shoulders by soft cords of cotton or silk, but never so loosely as to prove a nuisance to the swordsman.

The *kusadzuri*, or taces, is a light and efficient enough protector for the lower part of the body, but hardly as good as those in use in British gymnasiums. These are generally made of a tough cotton or hempen canvas, cut in five strips of about nine inches in length and four in width, two strips lying under, and three outside. Each of the strips is quilted, and bound round the edges with a leather. Though

46

hanging loose the strips are fastened to a band that encircles
the waist of the fencer, but in a way that does not impede
his movements in the slightest degree.

The *kote*, or gauntlet, is a hand, wrist, and forearm guard,
much superior, in many respects, to anything of the sort to

PRIOR TO THE SALUTE

be seen in our gymnasiums. A *kote* is made of strong
cotton or hempen canvas, lined with bamboo shavings or
horse-hair, and trimmed and strengthened with a soft, kid-
like leather. One great advantage the Japanese *kote* possesses
over our gauntlets is that its size can be regulated up to
quite an appreciable degree by the loosening or tightening
of the lacing running along and inside its forearm portion.

The *shinai*, or practice sword, is made from four strips of
bamboo, and though it undoubtedly looks clumsy enough at

47

first, it is not so by any means. The length and weight of
shinai vary according to the taste of fencers, there being no
rule laid down about this—surely a fairer method than ours,
which forces all men to use the same-sized practice sword,
irrespective of their stature and strength. The four strips of
bamboo being cut to fit each other are then brought together,
and over the grip or handle end of the *shinai* is drawn a strong
leather covering. The grip may be of any length, say from
eight to sixteen inches, or more. From the guard end of
this covering runs a leather or gut strand to the point of the
shinai, and is there fastened to a leather cup-like covering
that keeps together the ends of the four bamboos, and forms
a button over their points. The line along which the gut
runs is considered the back of the sword, and as the *shinai* is
strengthened and kept together by a fastening of leather at
its cutting point, advantage is taken of this to run the gut
through it, and so help to keep it all the tauter in its place.
The *tsuba*, or guard, is a circular piece of stout leather, with
a hole in its centre to permit of its being passed up and over
the grip until it reaches the hilt, where it forms a circular
guard, standing out from the *shinai* an inch, or a little more.
Sometimes, but not often, a fencer will use a secondary *tsuba*,
made of thin leather and padded like a cushion. This will
lie between his hand and the ordinary *tsuba*. The measure-
ments of my favourite *shinai* are: blade, twenty-six inches,
and grip fourteen inches. But it must be pointed out here
that I stand but a trifle over five feet six inches, and have
somewhat small hands.

The *hakama*, or divided skirt of the *samurai*, is a most
comfortable article of clothing, which, while it affords a

certain amount of protection to the legs and lower parts of
the body, does not in the least impede a fencer's movements.
It is light, airy, and cool, and might, with very great
advantage, be introduced into England, in a modified form,
for the use of young girls.

Japanese fencing-rooms are all built on more or less the

THE ENGAGE

same plan, and the Takanawa fencing-room was no exception
to this. It was about thirty feet in length and about half
that in width. Two of its sides were opened to the air, and
along its other two sides ran a raised platform, a couple of
feet or so above the floor of the fencing arena. The platform
was furnished with mats, and on cold days with fire-boxes,
and was used indiscriminately as galleries for spectators or
dressing and resting-rooms for the fencers. Such men as

liked to keep their fencing gear there could do so, hanging
the same up on pegs along the side of the gallery. Here it
must be pointed out that all Japanese fencers have their own
special kit, the fencing-room supplying nothing.

Two men agreeing to have a bout will, after donning their
kit, step into the arena, and squatting down in front of each
other, at about eight feet apart, will then proceed to salute
one another by a bow. Rising slowly they will put themselves into position with *shinai* crossing at engage, as shown
in the illustration.

To go into details over all the cuts, guards, and points of
a Japanese fencer's *répertoire* is not the object of this
article, but it is well to point out here that during a fifteen
years' experience of *kenjutsu* I remember seeing only one
man make use of a real back-handed stroke, and he—though
one of the best sworsdmen in Japan—took the idea, I fancy,
from seeing me use it. Another remarkable point about the
Japanese system of swordsmanship is that its votaries never
deliver a point except at the throat; but this is, perhaps,
to be explained by the fact that until the seventies armour was
largely used by them. This point even is more of a job than
a lunging thrust, and is delivered from below upwards, with
the very evident object of getting in between the gorget and
the upper part of the breastplate. Though highly scientific,
kenjutsu is a very rough-and-tumble sort of sword-play,
absolutely free from parade and all theatrical touches, but
wonderfully practical withal. As Japanese chivalry is most
uncompromisingly based upon the idea that all is fair in war,
so Japanese swordsmen resort to certain methods which are
highly reprehensible from our point of view. Such a thing

as giving another man a chance never appears to enter their heads; and so, should a fencer lose his *shinai*, or fail in any way, his adversary immediately takes advantage of this to push home his attack with all the greater vigour.

CORPS À CORPS À LA JAPONAISE

The cuts most in favour with Japanese swordsmen are mainly of the chopping order, and mostly delivered at the head and right wrist. Some few, however, pay particular attention to their adversary's stomach, and, if skilful swordsmen, these are the most difficult to tackle. The cuts at the

51

head and wrist can be delivered from the engage position, and in the case of the former this is done by slightly raising the *shinai*, stepping sharply forward, and as sharply bringing the *shinai* down upon the adversary's head with a chop that carries on. The wrist cut is made by a disengaging cut-over, with, if necessary, a sharp side tap against the adversary's *shinai* to throw it out of line. Both these cuts can be parried by a slight raising of the *shinai* and an outward twist of the wrist, and from both parries return cuts can be made at either head or wrist. Ordinarily Japanese fencers stand much closer to each other than do those of Europe, and it is truly remarkable what little space a couple of good native swordsmen require for a fight to the death. Some on the contrary are very fond of keeping well away, and, if not followed up and brought to close quarters, resort to a widely different mode of attack, consisting mainly of slashing cuts, first with one hand and then with the other, the changes being carried out with wonderful rapidity. The principal swinging cut can be delivered for either side of an opponent's head, but if he is a good swordsman it is a somewhat risky one to resort to, for he can reply to it by either a stop thrust or a stop cut at the head. The guard for it is a mere raising of the sword to a sufficient height and in the right line. There is only one form of hanging guard known to Japanese swordsmen, and it is seldom resorted to, for it makes a smart return a matter of great difficulty.

The Japanese inhabiting a mountainous country have from time immemorial accustomed themselves to fight more on foot than on horseback, while our knights of old, being differently situated, never fought on foot except and only

when absolutely obliged by circumstances to do so. That the
western systems of swordsmanship of the present day are relics
of the old knightly days there can be no manner of doubt.
The sword then was the weapon of the mounted man, of a
one-handed swordsman, and to be of real use to him it was
necessary it should be of a goodly length, but while a
mounted man can use a fairly heavy sword with considerable
effect and advantage, a dismounted man is distinctly handi-
capped by being armed with such a weapon. Courtly ways
succeeding knightly ways, men then took to wearing lighter
made swords, but as it was still considered more honourable
to fight on horseback than on foot, and as men could not for
ever be changing their swords, and as a thrusting sword was
just as effective under the newer conditions ruling the non-
wearing of armour, so the rapier eventually came more and more
into use in the West. With the rapier came the great reliance
the European swordsman puts on the point, and with it also
came the necessity for fighting on strictly straight lines in
contradistinction to lines which enable and permit the breaking
of ground by a rougher style of swordsmanship. To use the
point to the best advantage a lunging thrust is required, and
to deliver a lunging thrust aright it is essential that the
ground underfoot should be free of impedimenta, and also on
a plane. The existence of such conditions cannot, however,
be relied upon, and the consequence is the more the sword
approaches the rapier in construction the less suitable it is
for use on rough ground. Now the *katana* can be used as
well on rough as on smooth and level ground, but though a
wonderfully effective weapon it is by no means a perfect one,
nor is katana-play alone—pure and simple—a perfect system

of swordsmanship. Such can only be arrived at by making a new style of sword and instituting a new style of sword-play, combining in them all that is best in the swords of the West and the swords of the Far East, and in the methods employed in their use.

Some of the best points about *kenjutsu* are, that from every guard or parry some two or more different returns can be made, and that such guards or parries are more of a fending-off order than strictly stopping ones, thus allowing the returns to be made more quickly and the guards with less exertion. Again, neither strength nor length of reach are of such great advantage in *kenjutsu* as they are in our Western systems of sword-play, and so men of varying sizes and degrees of strength are brought on footings of greater equality when practising it than they would be with us. And then again, while just as scientific as our systems of sword-play, the Japanese system is a much less artificial one, and so with the majority of men less time would be required for picking up a knowledge of it.

Very naturally a good swordsman is held in high repute among the Japanese, but curiously enough a good sword smith is perhaps more so; and the names of such men as Amakune, Kamigé, Shinsoku, and Amaza of the very olden days, and Munéchika, Yasutsuna, Sanémori, Yukihira, and Yoshimitsu of the middle ages, are known to all educated subjects of the Mikado; and then as for Masamune, Yoshi-hiro, and Muramasa, their names are household words in every homestead of the land. The two best swordsmen I have met in Japan were Sakakibara and Henmi. The first

was a tall, rather slightly built man, but though a grand
swordsman, somewhat inclined to play to the gallery.
Henmi-san, on the other hand, was a most unobtrusive
individual, standing about five-feet-one, and quite the most
graceful moving man I have ever seen ; but though Sakakibara had a greater following among the general public of
Tokyo, there is little doubt Henmi was the better swordsman of the two. I have seen him, while fencing with a
first-class swordsman, stop all of a sudden, drop his *shinai*,
and then invite the other to attack him. But try as this
other might, he could seldom get a cut into him, for where
Henmi was the fraction of a second before, the spot would be
vacant.

The Japanese have always been very fond of giving names
to their swords, such names being usually derived from some
circumstance connected with their career. The "Grass-
mowing sword," for instance, the most highly prized of
all the swords of Japan, was so called because, when a brushwood fire threatened to destroy his army, Yamato Také
mowed down the intervening brushwood with it, and so
stopped the flames and saved his troops. Yamato Také,
it may here be mentioned, was the son of the Emperor Keiko,
71—131 A.D. The "Higé Kiri" and "Hizamaru" were
two famous swords belonging to the Minamoto family, and
owe their names to the fact that when they were tested on a
couple of criminals sentenced to decapitation, one cut through
the *hige* or beard of the victim after severing the head from
the body, while the second cut through the *hiza* or knee of
the other luckless wretch as he sat or squatted to receive his
death blow.

The following among other mottoes are sometimes found engraved on the hilt of Japanese swords :—

"There's nought 'twixt heaven and earth that man need fear who carries at his belt this single blade."

"One's fate is in the hands of heaven, but a skilful fighter does not meet with death."

"In one's last days one's sword becomes the wealth of one's posterity."

CHAPTER IV

Japanese Wrestling

Sumō and Jujutsu

FEW people are so keen about wrestling as the Japanese, who have for centuries past practised two distinct kinds—*sumō* and *jujutsu*. As regards the difference existing between the two, it is worth noting that this is something more than a mere difference of style as between two schools of the same art. For while the votaries of *sumō* rely as much upon their personal strength and weight of body as upon any knowledge they may possess of scientific grips and falls, those of *jujutsu* aim solely at overthrowing an opponent by highly reasoned-out yieldings of self, or as a Japanese would put it, " by yielding to strength." And then again, while the *sumōtori* are essentially professional wrestlers, recruited mainly from the lower strata of Japanese society, among the devotees of *jujutsu* muster men of birth and education, and often, too, of high social position and standing.

Without going into undue details as regards the history of wrestling in Japan, it may here be as well to point out that until thirty years ago the *sumōtori* ranked next in social matters to the *samurai*, the soldier nobility of old Japan, for it was considered that their profession was a semi-military one. Now, however, all this is changed, and, instead of living lives of ease and honour under the protecting ægis of some great feudal lord or high dignitary of State, the *sumōtori* of to-day have to content themselves with dangling after the

KAWADSU-NO-SABURO AND MATANO-NO-GORO, TWO CELEBRATED
WRESTLERS OF OLD

heels of some one of their country's erstwhile despised *shonin*, or "merchants." But fortunately for them and the cause of *sumō*, the "Wrestlers' Guild" is still well to the fore, and not only helps and succours them in trouble and sickness, but exercises over them and their calling a beneficent despotism not unlike that exercised by the Jockey Club over horse-racing in England. In days gone by the *sumōtori* enjoyed many privileges—such as immunity from bridge and ferry

MIGI-YOTTSU, OR "FOUR GRIPS." RIGHT HANDS INSIDE

tolls, and they could also claim the hire of post-horses at specially low rates. Theatres, booths at fairs, and other places of amusement were policed by them, and without the permission of their guild the managers of such exhibitions dared not open.

59

The " Wrestlers' Guild " has its headquarters in Tokyo, and the officers in charge of its affairs have always been recruited from the retired list of old wrestlers and umpires. Both *sumōtori* and umpires enter upon their calling when

A POSTURING EXERCISE FOR STRENGTHENING THE
THIGH MUSCLES

quite young, and in the generality of cases owe their first start in life to the benevolent influence of some famous wrestler or umpire. Once fairly started upon their career, however, they then come under the orders of the guild, and without the sanction of that august body no wrestler may compete in any tournament or match, with the result that such a thing as "selling a match" is an unknown thing among the *sumōtori* of Japan. While the umpires retain their family nomenclature, the wrestlers have professional names bestowed upon them, as, for instance, Taiho, or "Great Gun," Nishi-no-Ume, or "Western Ocean," &c., &c.,—all indicative of great size and strength. For the *sumōtori*, it may here be remarked, are all huge men, almost giants in comparison to the ruck of their fellow-countrymen, and yet despite of their great paunches and the lumps and rolls of fat that encase their bodies, they are not only enormously strong, but active withal. Curiously enough, the training of the *sumōtori* is in strict opposition to all theories held upon such subjects by English athletes and trainers, for not only do they eat and drink excessively, but also any kind of food or liquor they may fancy. And then, as regards their work outside of the ring, it consists mainly in butting at posts with their shoulders and chests, and in lifting and flinging about and catching weights in the shape of sacks of rice, sand, and the like. They also go through a good deal of posturing with a view to the loosening and suppling of their limbs, and, perhaps, too, as a sort of balancing practice.

A budding aspirant for umpire honours is generally a member of a family that has followed that calling for generations, and commences his study of palæstral matters under the supervision of a thoroughly trustworthy senior. When deemed sufficiently advanced he will be put to umpire practice bouts and the bouts of novices, and he gets his promotion according to vacancies and his own competency.

According to Japanese records, the first great umpire was
Shiga Seirin, who umpired the wrestling matches fought out
before the Emperor Shonin (724-749 A.D.). The baton of
office wielded by an umpire is a fan of the old time military
type; similarly antique is his costume. His orders and

A GROUP OF BUDDING ASPIRANTS FOR PALÆSTRAL HONOURS, WITH
A YOUNG UMPIRE STANDING AMONG THEM

injunctions to the wrestlers and his address to the spectators
are given in a peculiarly high-pitched tone, very dramatically
and very penetratingly. Ranking next to a *samurai*, and
often one, an umpire is allowed to wear a sword, and at all
great matches he invariably does so.

According to their skill so the *sumōtori* are divided into
classes, weight having nothing to do with the matter, and

the classifying of them is altogether in the hands of the guild. Their examinations for class honours are carried out twice a year, in January and May, within the famous temple grounds of Ekoin, in Tokyo, and excites immense enthusiasm among all classes of that great city's population. For days before the contest the streets are made noisier than

TACHI-AI, OR "WATCHING FOR AN OPENING"

usual by men beating drums, announcing the day and hour upon which the matches are to commence, and, besides all this, a great drumming is kept up on a specially prepared tower called a *Yagura*, standing some forty feet high and immediately in front of the wrestling booth. An amphitheatre having been erected, in the centre of it is left a square arena, and in the centre of this again is built up an eighteen feet square structure to a height of from two to four feet above the level of the ground. This is unrailed, though roofed over, the pillars supporting the roof being firmly planted at the four corners, and in the exact centre of all is pitched the wrestling ring, twelve feet in diameter, marked out by a plaited straw rope. The pillars and roof are adorned with draperies, flags, bannerets, &c., and the whole turn-out makes quite a brave show.

When all is ready a *toshiyori*, or elder from among the retired wrestlers, steps into the arena and declares the meeting opened, and the *sumōtori*, who are divided into two parties, then file into it from opposite sides. One party is invariably called the east and the other the west, and when they have finished filing in they squat down, the members of each party on their own side of the arena. Two of the least skilful of the contestants then step into the ring, one from each side, being ushered in by a junior umpire, who, after introducing them to the spectators by their professional names and status, orders them to commence. Being low down the grade of wrestlers, they, as also the half-a-dozen or so couples that follow immediately after, dispense with preliminaries, as much, perhaps, because of their ignorance of them as for any more valid reason. Not so, however, their seniors, who, after having been ushered into the ring and introduced to the spectators by an umpire of an equal status to themselves, proceed to go through some of the most fantastic and extraordinary posturings and pre- liminaries imaginable, winding up by taking a pinch of salt and tossing the same in the air as an oblation to Nomi-no- Sukune, the tutelary deity of the wrestlers of Japan.

64

A *mawashi*, or "loin cloth," is all that covers a *sumōtori's* nakedness while actually engaged in a bout. It is generally made of hemp, but sometimes of silk, and may be either white or red in colour. The aprons worn during posturing

DO-HYO-IRI, OR "CEREMONIAL APRON," AS WORN BY
FIRST-CLASS JAPANESE WRESTLERS

and preliminaries by the highest ranked *sumōtori* are the Japanese equivalents of a British pugilist's belt, and being richly embroidered in gold and silk sometimes cost as much as 1,000 *yen*, equal to about £100. *Sumōtori* invariably allow their hair to grow as long as possible, shaving off, however, a portion of it in front, and tying it back into a queue fasten it on the top and back of their heads.

When both wrestlers have done with their preliminaries they take up their positions within and on opposite sides

SIKI-KABURI. A BACK THROW FOILED

of the ring. Squatting on their haunches they watch for an opening, and when one of them sees it he immediately makes a dart at the other, but the chances are his opponent will not recognise it as a fair start. This may occur over and over again, but once fairly started a Japanese wrestling bout is a very short-lived affair indeed, seldom lasting over a minute, and the reason is that the men are as often as not afraid to grapple for fear of being pushed, butted, or thrown

A GROUP OF FAMOUS WRESTLERS, INCLUDING EX-CHAMPION
AND PRESENT CHAMPION OF JAPAN

out of the ring before they have well commenced. For, as has been already pointed out, the ring is but twelve feet in diameter, and the least possible throw, step or push outside of it loses a *sumōtori* his bout and perhaps his rank and status also, and this means money to him, for according to their rank and status so the men are paid.

There are forty-eight recognised methods or hands for coping with an antagonist, and the Japanese claim they have remained unchanged for centuries. In addition to these, there are a hundred and sixty-eight possible or subsidiary hands. The orthodox hands are classified into throwing, grappling, twisting and bending, each having twelve hands, but these do not, of course, exhaust a good wrestler's resources, which, within certain bounds, depend upon his quickness of eye and decision. Should a wrestler employ methods dangerous to life and limb he is at once admonished, and should he do so again he is promptly ejected from out the arena and the guild, and this is a punishment that carries with it penalties similar in all respects to the suspension of a jockey by the Jockey Club of England.

In the first rank of the *sumōtori* stand the Ozeki, then the Sekiwaki and Komusubi. Following them come seven gradations or classes of Mayegashira. Should an Ozeki prove himself superior to all his rivals of the same rank he is promoted to Hinoshita Kaizan, carrying with it the privilege of wearing the *yohozuka*, or "side rope," a belt in the form of a rope. According to Japanese accounts Akashi Shigenosuke was the first to have this honour conferred upon him, in 1624 A.D., and since his time there have been only sixteen *kaizan*, the latest being Hitachiyama, the present champion of Japan.

Jujutsu

As before explained, *jujutsu* is a very different art to *sumō*, ranking considerably higher than it in the esteem of the more aristocratic portions of Japanese society. Its principles,

like so many other things Japanese, were until lately handed
down as a sort of esoteric secret from one great master of the
art to another, and, unlike as in the case of *sumō*, there are
many schools or styles of *jujutsu*. It is essentially a military
art, and in the feudal days instructions in it formed a no
mean part in the education of a young *samurai*. For some

KO-MATA-DORI, OR " LEG-PULL THROW "

time after the abolition of the feudal system it looked as if
it was going to become one of the many lost arts, but happily
for the future prospects of Japanese manhood a revival took
place, and at present it is extremely popular among all classes
of the Mikado's subjects.   *Jujutsu* is known to the Japanese
under various names, such as *judo, yawara, taijutsu, kogusoku,
kempo* and *hakuda*, but *judo, jujutsu* and *yawara* are the

69

terms most commonly used. Considering the high esteem in
which it has always been held, it is really wonderful what few
books there are upon it, and still more wonderful that such as
there are have not dealt as fully with it as they might have.
Such books, or rather pamphlets, as have dealt with it have

KATA-SUKASHI, A SIDE-SLIP FOLLOWED BY A NECK-GRIP THROW

generally so done from the particular standpoint of some one
of the many schools of *jujutsu*, and there is absolutely no
doubt the originators of certain new schools have made
history to suit their own purpose. Still, there seems little
doubt that, while *kogusoku* and *kempo* were originally two
distinct arts, the former the art of *seizing* and the latter the
art of *gaining victory by pliancy*, the two were afterwards

amalgamated and formed into one art and that *jujutsu* as we now know it. As to the date when *jujutsu* first became firmly established as an art necessary to the proper training of a warrior, that would appear to have been somewhere about the middle of the seventeenth century. A Chinese refugee

SETTING-TO

named Chingempin had apparently something to do with its introduction into Japan, for his name appears in nearly every pamphlet bearing upon the subject from a historical point of view. But for all that the art, like so many others originally borrowed from the Chinese, is now essentially Japanese.

To explain straight off what *jujutsu* is would indeed puzzle any one, for it stands in somewhat the same category toward wrestling as fencing does toward single-stick practice, and it is again an art of fighting without weapons on lines entirely distinct from those followed by the pugilists of England and

TAI-OTOSHI, OR "STANDING SIDE-THROW"

America, or by the *savate* players of France. An expert at *jujutsu* has, figuratively speaking, many cards up his sleeve,— he can throw an opponent heavily enough to daze, to stun or to kill him; he can choke, strangle or throttle him with his bare hands, arms, legs, or even by twisting his clothing tightly around his neck; he can hold him down on the ground, or in such a position as to render him absolutely helpless, or he can twist and bend his arms, legs or fingers so as to force him to give in through sheer pain.

The different schools of *jujutsu* practise all these various methods of overcoming an opponent, but it is only in some of them, that *atemi* and *kuatsu* are taught. *Atemi* is the art of striking or kicking some particular part of an opponent's body in order to kill, injure, or incapacitate him from further resistance. *Kuatsu*, which means to "resuscitate," is taught only to a favoured few for the purpose of resuscitating those who have apparently died through violence. The methods employed by the practisers of *kuatsu* are many and differ considerably according to the schools, but the one most commonly employed when a man has been stunned by a fall or blow is to embrace the patient firmly from behind and just under the armpits, to then lift him up to a standing position and to raise him up and down sharply once or twice, allowing his feet to strike the ground each time, and it is truly remarkable how very often and how very efficacious this generally is.

In days gone by the *samurai* learnt *jujutsu* with the same spirit and object in view as they learnt to use a sword, but of late it has been developed into a system of athletics and mental and moral training, and as such it undoubtedly is of inestimable value to the youths of Japan. In the best equipped schools in Tokyo daily instructions are carried out by means of lectures on the theory of the art as well as by actual practice; and, as the best teachers of it so justly claim,

a knowledge of it gives confidence to men and helps them to
face dangers and difficulties in a proper and manly spirit, and
in illustration of this they tell many amusing and instructive

HIKI-OTOSHI, OR " PULL-DOWN THROW "

stories.   That of Terada Goyemon must here suffice : Terada
lived in Tokyo some forty years ago, in days when it was
considered necessary for princes and high officers of state to
be accompanied by bands of armed retainers whenever they

showed themselves in public. Being out one day on some business, Terada fell in with the procession of the Prince of Mito, and the *sakibarai*, or attendants of the Prince, while making way for the procession ordered him to kneel down, which he refused to do, explaining that a *samurai* of his rank did not require to kneel unless the Prince's *kago*, or " sedan-chair," came nearer. The *sakibarai*, however, persisted in their endeavours to force him to kneel, and five or six of them attempted to throw him down, but he freed himself and threw them all to the ground. Other *sakibarai* coming up threatened to kill him, but he threw them down too, and seizing their *jittei*, small iron rods or maces, ran over to the Prince's *yashiki*, or official residence, saying : " I am a *samurai* of such and such a rank, and it is against the dignity of my feudal lord that I should kneel down. I regret that I had to throw your men down, but I had to do it to preserve my honour, and here are the *jittei* which I return to you." To the credit of the Prince be it said, he was so pleased with Terada that he asked him to enter his service. This, however, that true *samurai* refused to do, claiming that his place was by his own Prince's side.

As regards the present mania in England for *jujutsu*—and may it increase and live long—it is just as well to point out here that though the art is undoubtedly a most scientific one, yet if people will only think for a moment they will realise how very absurd and sensational are some of the claims advanced upon its behalf. Time and again I have been asked how a good *jujutsu* man would shape in front of a first-class boxer, and the only answer I have ever been able to give is that it would depend entirely upon the individual exponents of their own peculiar art. There is no neater fighter in existence than a good boxer, and if such a one got home with his blow first he would most probably knock his man

KEKAISHI, OR "KICK-BACK THROW"

down, if not out; but if he bungled over the affair in the slightest degree the *jujutsu* man would, or should, be in to him at once, and then there can be little doubt the result would be all in his favour. But when talking of *jujutsu* and boxing, comparing the one with the other, people either forget or are unaware that while the majority of Japanese make a perfect study of their own peculiar art, few Englishmen do so of theirs. The result is that skilled *jujutsu* men exist in far greater numbers among the Japanese than skilled boxers do among Englishmen. And then again, to be thoroughly sure of knocking out his man cleanly and efficiently, a boxer must be up to professional form, while a *jujutsu* man, on the other hand, and one, moreover, who need by no means be any great expert, can easily throw and incapacitate any man, except, and only, another and superior exponent of his art. As an auxiliary to fisticuffs and swordplay *jujutsu* certainly ranks high ; that is to say, if one regards and practices those two grand arts from a practical standpoint—as arts of offence and defence rather than of mere physical exercise.

As a physical exercise, pure and simple, there is, however, much to be said in favour of *jujutsu*, for victory does not depend upon a mere question of avoirdupois and brute force, as must be admitted to be the case with the majority of our native arts of offence and self-defence. In fact, the art of *jujutsu* is more mental than muscular, and might well be described as the mathematics of all physical exercises, on such wonderfully exact lines is it based. Balance being the key-note of *jujutsu*, the result of its teachings is a well-balanced and graceful carriage of the body when standing and when walking, and, it may also be added, when falling, and when getting up from a fall, for how to fall properly is the first thing taught an aspirant for *jujutsu* honours. The result of such teachings is that a student of the art, whether man,

77

woman, or child, soon gains so perfect a control over his or
her muscular system as to help minimise, to a wonderful

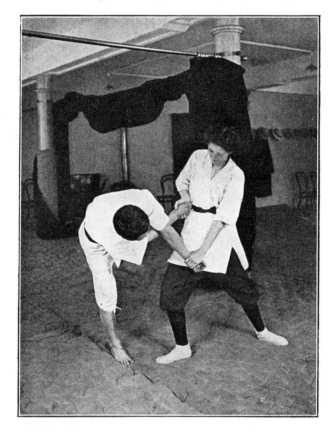

MISS ROBERTS, LADY INSTRUCTRESS, THE JAPANESE SCHOOL
OF JUJUTSU, APPLYING THE "ARM-BREAK LOCK"

extent, dangers from accidents which might otherwise prove
serious, if not fatal; such, for instance, as so often occur at
crossings in the more crowded streets of London; and all

this is gained without any undue hardening and mis-shaping of the muscles.

In conclusion, it may be as well here to point out that it is by no means necessary for an intending student of *jujutsu* to be an athlete, rather the other way; for such athletes, unfortunately, when commencing a course of *jujutsu*, are inclined to rely overmuch on their strength and activity, a fatal mistake if one hopes to attain to any degree of proficiency in the art. Unlike those muscle-trying exercises which necessitate the use of developers, dumb-bells, bar-bells, &c. (from the sale of which such enormous profits are derived by the proprietors of certain much-vaunted and advertised schools of physical culture), *jujutsu* is a natural art, an unartificial exercise, and one which, partly by reason of its superiority to all extraneous appliances, affords the very healthiest fun, emulation, and exercise in existence.

THE END